7

STUNT PROS

Frances Ridley

with thanks to Steve Truglia

Crabtree Publishing Company

www.crabtreebooks.com

CAFÉ

Crabtree Publishing Company

www.crabtreebooks.com   1-800-387-7650
Copyright © **2009 CRABTREE PUBLISHING COMPANY**.

**Published
in Canada
Crabtree Publishing**
616 Welland Ave.
St. Catharines, ON
L2M 5V6

**Published in the
United States
Crabtree Publishing**
PMB16A
350 Fifth Ave., Suite 3308
New York, NY   10118

Content development by Shakespeare Squared
www.ShakespeareSquared.com

Every effort has been made to trace copyright holders, and we apologize in advance for any omissions. We would be pleased to insert the appropriate acknowledgments in any subsequent edition of this publication.

Author: Frances Ridley
Project editor: Ruth Owen
Project designer: Simon Fenn
Photo research: Ruth Owen
Project coordinator: Robert Walker
Production coordinator: Katherine Berti
Prepress technicians: Samara Parent,
    Katherine Berti, Ken Wright

Thank you to
Lorraine Petersen
and the members
of nasen

Picture credits:
Barcroft Media: p. 21
Big Pictures: p. 25 (bottom), 29
Breakaway Effects Ltd: p. 16–17
Corbis: Bettmann: p. 11 (bottom), 12; Rick Doyle: p. 4, 5
Corbis Sygma: p. 9 (bottom), 13
Sophia Crawford: p. 27
Getty Images: p. 6 (bottom), 28
Peter Hassall: p. 22, 23
Kristoffer Jorgensen: p. 8, 15 (top), 15 (center)
Scot Leva, Precisionstunts.com: p. 7 (top and bottom)
Rex Features: 20th Century Fox/Everett: p. 27 (inset); Denis
    Cameron: front cover; Everett Collection: p. 9 (top), 11 (top),
    24; Simon Roberts: p. 26 (main); Charles Sykes: p. 26 (inset)
RGA: p. 10; United Artists: p. 25 (top)
Shutterstock: p. 1, 2–3, 4–5 (background), 8 (background), 12–13
    (background), 14 (right), 18–19 (background), 19 (top), 20, 31
Steve Truglia, Prostunts.net: p. 14 (left), 18, 19 (bottom)
wikimedia commons: p. 6 (top)

Library and Archives Canada Cataloguing in Publication

Ridley, Frances
        Stunt pros / Frances J. Ridley.

(Crabtree contact)
Includes index.
ISBN 978-0-7787-3779-7 (bound).--ISBN 978-0-7787-3801-5 (pbk.)

        1. Stunt performers--Juvenile literature.
I. Title. II. Series: Crabtree contact

PN1995.9.S7R53 2009   j791.4302'8   C2008-907861-6

Library of Congress Cataloging-in-Publication Data

Ridley, Frances.
    Stunt pros / Frances J. Ridley.
        p. cm. -- (Crabtree contact)
    Includes index.
    ISBN 978-0-7787-3801-5 (pbk. : alk. paper) -- ISBN 978-0-
7787-3779-7 (reinforced library binding : alk. paper)
    1. Stunt performers--Juvenile literature. 2. Daredevils--Juvenile
literature. I. Title. II. Series.

PN1995.9.S7R54 2009
791.4302'8092--dc22
                                                              2008052391

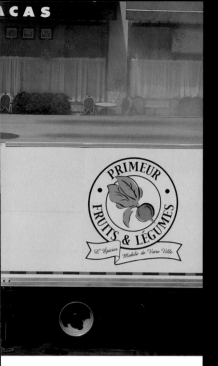

CONTENTS

Chapter 1
Action!

Chapter 2
Movie Stunts Timeline

Chapter 3
Stunt Stars

Chapter 4
A Career in Stuntwork

Chapter 5
Stunts and Safety

Chapter 6
Super Stunts

Chapter 7
Stunt Doubles

Chapter 8
007 Stunts

Need-to-know Words

Getting into Stunt Work/
Stunts Online

Index

CHAPTER 1
ACTION!

Action movies are exciting to watch! An action hero leaps from a burning building. A car flies through the air and smashes into a truck!

It looks as if the actors do these stunts. In fact, most stunts are performed by stuntmen and women.

Stunt performers take the place of actors. They perform stunts that are too difficult or too dangerous for the actors to do.

Stuntman Greg Brazzell drives a car into a truck filled with water bottles

CHAPTER 2

MOVIE STUNTS TIMELINE

1900s to 1930s

At first, Hollywood actors performed their own stunts in their movies. Audiences loved these action scenes. Film **directors** soon began to use stunt performers.

Rose Wenger was a **rodeo** rider. She **doubled** for an actress called Helen Holmes in a Western movie serial.

Rose Wenger

1940s to 1950s

Film directors wanted more amazing stunts.

Performers developed ways to make stunts as safe as possible.

They used trampolines, cardboard boxes, and straw to break the high falls.

New technology was developed to make stunts look more real. **Air rams** and **air bags** were invented.

Air rams throw a performer into the air.

Air ram

1980s TO 1990s

Action films, such as *Rambo, Indiana Jones,* and *Die Hard,* became very popular. They were packed with stunts and **special effects**.

A member of a stunt crew tests a flying vest

Many films used wire work stunts.
The performers fly through the air on wires.

 If you do CGI and real stunt work together, you can do fantastic things.

Joel Silver, Hollywood Producer

2000s

Many film directors now use computers to make realistic action scenes. But real stunts are still popular!

The Matrix movies mix **computer generated imagery** (CGI), wire work, and **martial arts**.

Wires

Green screen

The actors were filmed against a green screen.
Then a background was added using a computer.
Wires were removed by computer, too.
The actors look as if they are flying above the ground.

CHAPTER 3 STUNT STARS

Buster Keaton
Lived 1895 to 1966

Buster Keaton was a silent film actor.
He did many of his own stunts. In this
famous scene, a house falls on Keaton.
The house misses Keaton because he is
standing below an open window.

Yakima Canutt
Lived 1895 to 1986

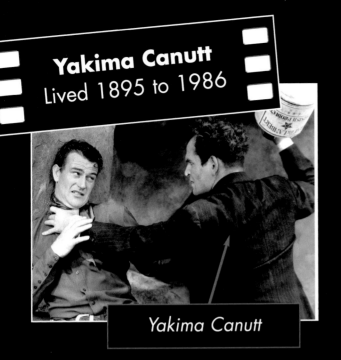

Yakima Canutt

Canutt did his first film stunt in 1915. He got his last film **credit** in 1975! Canutt and his friend, the actor John Wayne, developed fighting and stunt **techniques**.

Pearl White
Lived 1889 to 1938

Pearl White was an actress who did many of her own stunts. She starred in *The Perils of Pauline*.

Her most famous stunt was when she was tied to railroad tracks in front of a speeding train!

Robinson does tricks on a trampoline hanging from a helicopter

In 1980, Dar Robinson jumped off the CN Tower in Toronto, Canada. He did this stunt for the movie *High Point.* His hidden parachute opened just 295 feet (90 m) from the ground!

Dar Robinson liked to set stunt records. He was the first person to skydive out of a plane at 11,811 feet (3,600 m) while riding in a small sports car.

CN Tower

Jackie Chan started his career as a stuntman in **Bruce Lee** Kung Fu movies.

Chan's movies mix comedy with Kung Fu action.

15

CHAPTER 4
A CAREER IN STUNTWORK

This is Steve Truglia. He is a stunt performer and stunt coordinator. Stunt coordinators plan the stunts for action scenes in movies and TV shows.

> " Today I'm planning a fight scene for a new movie. The stunt must look real but it must also be as safe as possible. "

Steve Truglia

PLANNING A STUNT

- I read the **script** and make notes on the action scenes.

- I discuss how the stunt should look with the film director.

- I work out how much the stunt will cost.

- I visit the film **location**. This is called a "recce."

- I choose the stunt performers.

14

On the day of a shoot, the stunt performers practice the stunt.

In a stunt fight, the performer's hand never makes contact with the face.

Skilled stunt performers and clever **camera angles** make a stunt fight look real.

A good stunt is based on strong teamwork. Often, on big movies, a separate film crew works on the action scenes. This is called the "Second Unit."

❝ When I'm planning a stunt, safety is everything. I have to think what if... **❞**

Steve Truglia

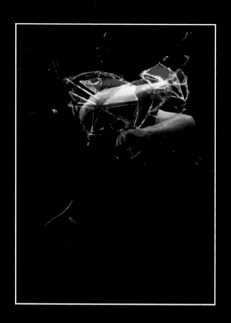

In the fight scene, one of the stunt performers will be thrown through a window.

Film sets have windows and items such as bottles made from special materials. These materials smash easily and safely. They are known as "breakaway effects."

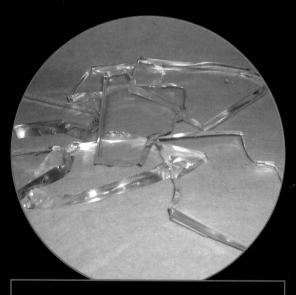

This is rubber glass. It can be torn or crumbled into pieces.

16

A stuntman crashes through breakaway glass

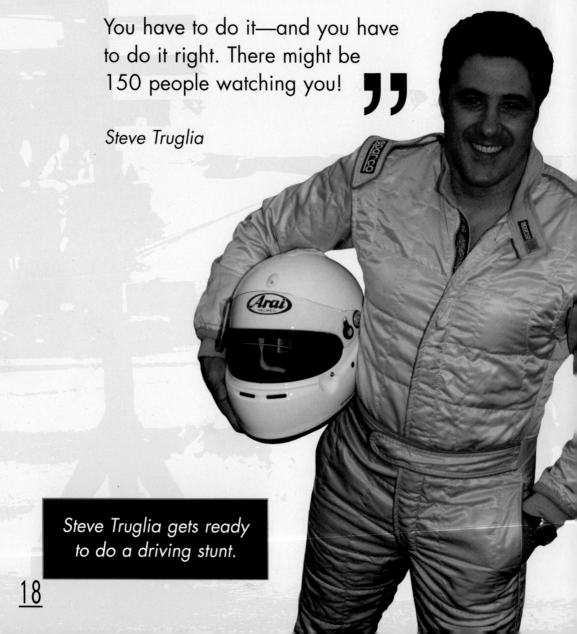

"People who take risks don't make good stunt performers.

I'm a very careful person. I make sure that my stunts are set up as safely as possible. I practice my stunts before I perform them.

The last few minutes before I perform a stunt are tense. There is a lot of pressure.

You have to do it—and you have to do it right. There might be 150 people watching you!"

Steve Truglia

Steve Truglia gets ready to do a driving stunt.

Stuntmen and women learn to drive at high speeds. They learn how to skid, spin, and even drive on two wheels!

" When you perform a stunt, you must focus on the stunt. Nothing matters but what you're doing! "

Steve Truglia

This car "knock-down" stunt is dangerous. Steve plans every second and practices every move he makes.

STUNTS
AND SAFETY

Many movies have scenes where people are on fire. These are called burn scenes. They are very dangerous to perform.

The stunt performers wear fireproof clothes. They use a special gel to stop their skin and hair from burning.

The performers must not breathe when they are on fire. They could burn their lungs or breathe in poisonous fumes.

The burn is carefully timed. People trained to give medical help stand by, in case of an emergency. The stunt crew is ready to put out the fire.

Stuntman Steve Truglia performs a fire burn

21

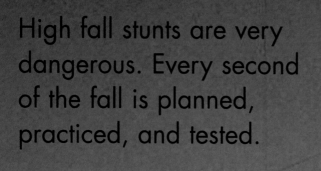

High fall stunts are very dangerous. Every second of the fall is planned, practiced, and tested.

Stunt performers learn how to fall and how to land.

If a stunt performer lands in the wrong position, he or she can be badly hurt.

Air bag

Giant air bags give stunt performers a
safe place to land during "high fall" stunts.

A "safety spotter" keeps watch from out
of view of the camera. Safety spotters are
normally other stunt performers.

If a stunt performer gets into trouble,
the spotter is ready to help.

A safe landing

The person jumping knows that everything
is safe. However, he or she still needs the
courage to jump!

CHAPTER 6 SUPER STUNTS

Stunt performers are always pushing themselves to the limit.

The 1959 movie *Ben Hur* features a Roman chariot race. Yakima Canutt directed the race. His son Joe was one of the stunt performers.

The chariot race in Ben Hur

During the race, Joe Canutt's chariot was bumped by another chariot. He nearly fell out. Canutt could have been crushed by the racing chariots.

The bump was planned, but Canutt's near fatal fall wasn't!

Bud Ekins was Steve McQueen's double for this scene from *The Great Escape*.

Ekins had to jump a motorcycle over a barbed wire fence.

Sébastien Foucan is a parkour expert. Parkour involves running, jumping, and climbing over obstacles such as buildings.

Sébastien Foucan

Foucan starred in the opening chase scene from the James Bond movie, *Casino Royale*.

CHAPTER 7 | STUNT DOUBLES

Stunt co-ordinators choose stunt performers for two important reasons:
- They are trained and **insured** to do the stunt.
- They are good doubles for the actor.

Debbie Evans is a top Hollywood stuntwoman. She is also a champion motorcycle rider.

Carrie-Anne Moss

Debbie Evans was the stunt double for actress Carrie-Anne Moss in The Matrix Reloaded.

Most stunt performers get paid by the day or by the week. Some performers get **contracts** for longer periods of time.

Sophia Crawford got a contract for a complete TV series. She was the stunt double for Sarah Michelle Gellar in 78 episodes of *Buffy the Vampire Slayer*.

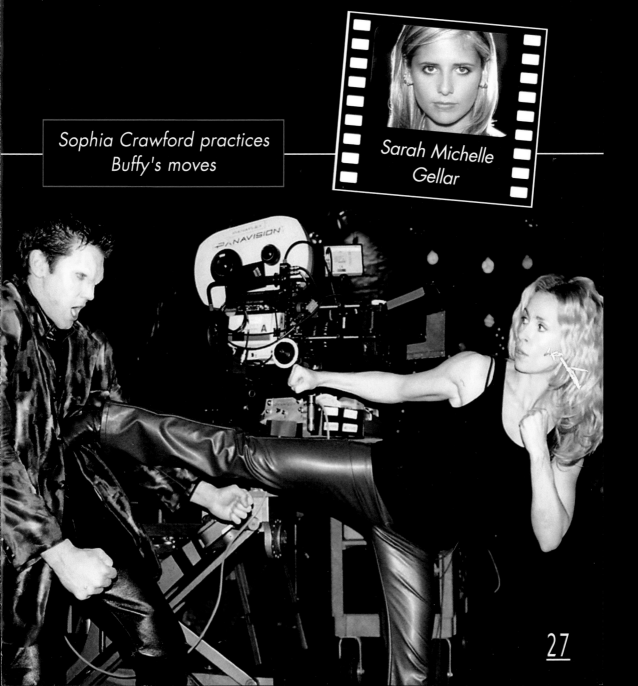

Sophia Crawford practices
Buffy's moves

Sarah Michelle
Gellar

CHAPTER 8

007 STUNTS

Not all actors need a stunt double all of the time! Daniel Craig is the latest actor to play James Bond.

In *Casino Royale* and *Quantum of Solace*, Craig wanted to perform as many of his own stunts as possible.

In *Casino Royale* the stunts included a stair fall and an underwater rescue scene. Craig got bruises and cuts and even lost a tooth.

" If you don't get bruised playing Bond, you're not doing it properly.

Daniel Craig **"**

Wire

Padding

Craig leaps from a rooftop
in Quantum of Solace

NEED-TO-KNOW WORDS

air bag A giant bag filled with air. It provides a safe place to land

air ram A piece of equipment that throws a performer up into the air

Bruce Lee A martial arts expert who made martial arts popular in movies

camera angle The position from which the camera shoots the film

computer generated imagery (CGI) Realistic-looking images that have been created using a computer

contract An agreement, in law, between people

credit When a person's name is shown at the end of a film

director The person who chooses the actors and tells them what to do in each scene of a movie, play, or TV show. The director also decides how the cameras should film the scenes

double Someone who takes an actor's place in a movie

insured If you are insured it means you have paid money into a fund in case something bad happens to you. If something bad does happen, the fund pays money to help you

location The place where a movie or TV show is filmed

martial arts Ways of fighting without weapons, such as Kung Fu, karate, and judo

rodeo A contest in which cowboys show off their horse-riding skills

script The words the actors say in a movie, play, or TV show

special effects Tricks that movie-makers use to make the audience think that something is real in a movie

technique A way of doing something

GETTING INTO STUNT WORK

Here are some tips for getting into stunt work.

- You will need good physical fitness. Stunt performers take part in sports that are good for all-round fitness, such as running and swimming.

- Stunt performers need useful skills such as martial arts, rock climbing, skydiving, or riding motorcycles or horses.

- Try getting work as a film extra (for example a person in a crowd scene). This helps you to get a license to work in films and on TV. It's also a good way to find out about film sets and to meet stunt co-ordinators.

STUNTS ONLINE

www.prostunts.net/home.htm
News and views from professional stuntman Steve Truglia

www.skillset.org/film/jobs/performing/article_4712_1.asp
Find out how to be a stunt performer

en.wikipedia.org/wiki/Dar_Robinson
Find out more about stuntman Dar Robinson

INDEX

A
air bags 7, 22-23, 30
air rams 7, 30

B
Ben Hur 24
Bond, James 25, 28–29
breakaway effects 16–17
Buffy the Vampire Slayer 27

C
Canutt, Joe 24
Canutt, Yakima 11, 24
car stunts 19
Casino Royale 25, 28
Chan, Jackie 13
computer generated (CGI)
    stunts 8–9, 30
Craig, Daniel 28–29
Crawford, Sophia 27

D
doubles 26–27, 30

E
Ekins, Bud 25
Evans, Debbie 26

F
fight scenes 14–15
fire burns 20–21
Foucan, Sébastien 25

G
Gellar, Sarah Michelle 27
green screens 9

H
high falls 6, 22–23
High Point 12
History of stuntwork 6–7

K
Keaton, Buster 10

L
Lee, Bruce 13, 30

M
Matrix, The (movies) 9
Matrix Reloaded, The 26
McQueen, Steve 25
Moss, Carrie-Anne 26

P
parkour 25
Perils of Pauline, The 11

Q
Quantum of Solace 29

R
Robinson, Dar 12

S
safety 6, 14–15, 18–19, 20,
    22–23
stunt co-ordinators 14–15, 26

T
training 31
Truglia, Steve 14–15, 18–19, 21

W
Wayne, John 11
Wenger, Rose 6
White, Pearl 11
wire work stunts 8–9, 29

Printed in the U.S.A. - BG